J. R Walker

Eddyism

Christian Science Neither Christian nor Scientific

J. R Walker

Eddyism
Christian Science Neither Christian nor Scientific

ISBN/EAN: 9783337417215

Printed in Europe, USA, Canada, Australia, Japan

Cover: Foto ©Lupo / pixelio.de

More available books at **www.hansebooks.com**

EDDYISM;

OR,

Christian Science Neither Christian Nor Scientific.

BY

REV. J. R. WALKER,

Synodical Missionary of Pacific Synod, Cumberland
Presbyterian Church.

———————

NASHVILLE, TENN.:

THE CUMBERLAND PRESS.

1899.

PREFATORY NOTE.

In my dealing with Christian Scientists and those favorably impressed by their tenets, I have recognized the need of just such a book as this. While recognizing much that is meritorious, all I have seen written against Christian Science has failed to give a comprehensive view of it including sufficient quotations from its founder's writings. The quotations herein are numerous and necessarily fragmentary. Those from Mrs. Eddy's book, "Science and Health," are followed by the page number in parenthesis, and are taken from the edition of 1896. There are a few quotations from two of her other books, "Pulpit and Pew" and "Unity of Good."

May this book be blessed of God in breaking the force of this strangely popular and unreasonable error.   J. R. WALKER.

Fresno, Cal.

CONTENTS.

CONTENTS

INTRODUCTION.

I approach the treatment of this subject with much trepidation.

First, because of the difficulty of understanding it. The literature of Christian Science is mystical, obscure, and contradictory. I have read much of it, and have talked much with those who teach and follow it. I have given special attention to that fountain of authority, "Science and Health," by Mrs. Mary Baker G. Eddy. This book is certainly honored with a place alongside the Bible by most well-informed Christian Scientists. In reality, it is given superior authority, for even the plain teachings of the Holy Scriptures are made to bend to the fantastic spiritualizations of "Science and Health." This book of 663 pages, counting the index, I have perused carefully and repeatedly. There are portions of it baptized with the spirit of devoutness. Much of it is hazy and utterly unintelligible. Much of it is contradictory. In one place the author appears to teach one thing; in another the opposite. Much of it is bombastic puerility. Mr. Walcott, who has written a treatise on this unique volume, truly says of it: "It appears to be beneath criticism, since it is written without a trace of literary art, and is without a single redeeming grace of style to relieve the tedium of disjointed, inconsequential, dogmatic, and egotistical assertion and repetition. One may open the book almost at random and read in either direction without materially modifying the character of the argument or the sequence of ideas." Yet the book sells by the thousands at a high price. To draw from this conglomerated mass the genuine gist, and present it in systematic form, is a task whose difficulty can be appreciated only by those who have undertaken it.

Second, I fear that the exposure of the silly idiosyncrasies of the system, along with the deadly error, may wound the feelings of some good people who permit themselves to be called Christian Scientists without knowing its dangerous tendency. There is also a fear that many intelligent people who have never investigated it may consider my description an overdrawn picture. To all such I would say, Read Mrs. Eddy's books, along with her magazine articles and those of her followers, and I am sure you will decide that I have done no injustice.

Mrs. Eddy claims to be the originator of the system. She says: "In the year 1866 I discovered the science of metaphysical healing and named it Christian Science" (1). "No human

tongue or pen taught me the science contained
in this book " (4). But the friends of Mr. P. P.
Quimby, a clairvoyant doctor, cite the fact that
while Mrs. Eddy was sick in 1862 she was
treated by him. He died in 1866 and his friends
persistently affirm that what Mrs. Eddy claims
to have discovered in 1866 was originated by
him. As is usually the case with error when
industriously disseminated, it has made rapid
headway. The number of adherents is now
estimated all the way from 200,000 to 700,000.
They have 300 church buildings, most of them
beautiful edifices. The building of the mother
church in Boston cost $240,000.

This rapid growth is due to the following con-
siderations :

1. The astounding claims of the system relative to bodily healing. Sick people, like a
drowning man, grasp at straws. After one has
suffered with bodily ailments for years, and has
consulted many physicians and paid out much
money without avail, it is not a great wonder if
he puts his case in the hands of one who says,
"I can heal you entirely without medicine or
compliance with any sanitary laws." And when
he recovers he is easily led into accepting the
whole system, donning the high-sounding name,
"Christian Scientist." Nor is it a wonder that
each case of healing has its local influence in

winning the adherence of some, the favorable
consideration of others, and silencing the opposition of others.

2. Mysticism. Christian Science draws around
it the robes of mystery. It has infused into it
the occultism of Theosophy. This appeals
strongly to many minds; and it cannot be denied that mystery has its influence on all. We
are curious to know the unknowable or that
which is difficult to know. The obscure language of Mrs. Eddy appears to contain a meaning dark and deep. It may be dark, but it is
rarely deep. Not all muddy water is deep. A
man was persuaded by some boys to try to dive
to the bottom of a pond in which they had been
wading. He was soon in mud head first to his
shoulders. A noted preacher defines meta-
physics as *muddy physics.* This is certainly true
of Mrs. Eddy's. The following are examples of
murkiness from Mrs. Eddy's writings: "Mind
is the grand creator, and there can be no power,
except that which is derived therefrom. If
Mind was first chronologically, is first potential-
ly, and must be first eternally, then give to
Mind the glory, honor, dominion, and power
everlastingly due unto its holy name. Inferior
and unspiritual methods of healing may try to
make Mind and medicine coalesce, but the two
will not mingle harmoniously" (37). From the

obscurity in this passage at least one thought gleams: Mrs. Eddy's god is an *it*.

The second example is from Mrs. Eddy's book, "Unity of Good," p. 14: "He (Jesus) said, 'The kingdom of heaven is here, and is included in Mind.' He declared, 'Ye say there are yet four months, and *then* cometh the harvest; but I say, Look up, not down, for your fields are already white for the harvest; and gather the harvest by mental, not material, processes. The laborers are few in the vineyard of Mind-sowing and reaping; but let them apply to the waving grain the curving sickle of Mind's eternal circle, and bind it with bands of soul." Rather ethereal grain harvesting, and that from a vineyard!

Mrs. Eddy as a Bible student is certainly the peer of the ex-preacher who boasted of his Bible knowledge and requested a friend of mine to preach a sermon on "David's stirring words uttered when hemmed in the cave by the Philistines: 'I am now ready to be offered, and the time of my departure is at hand. I have fought a good fight,'" etc.

The reader will please pardon one more instance from Mrs. Eddy's book, "Pulpit and Press," p. 7: "Is not a man metaphysically and mathematically number one, a unit, and therefore whole number, governed and protected by his

divine principle, God? You have simply to pre-
serve a scientific, positive sense of unity with
your divine source and daily demonstrate this."

These quotations remind me of a Fourth of July
address, the opening sentence of which was:
" This is a world of equipoise and intelligence,
and the brute advocates the adversary." De-
scribing the rapid growth of the West, the
speaker seriously assured his audience that " the
wind sighs in dithyrambic requiems through the
suple-jacks of the forest, where nature is sprous-
ing in her first attitudes." While there is much
in the grandiloquent mysticism of Mrs. Eddy's
writings to strike with awe the uneducated, an
intelligent attempt at analyzation will usually
end in disgust or laughter.*

3. It accepts the Bible and copies after the
Church. This appeals to Christians and those
favorable to true religion. It is true, its vague
and shadowy interpretations of the holy Book
are such as to work an entire transformation in
its import, but this is not always apparent to the
uninitiated and novitiate.

---

* The following is a passage quoted approvingly on one of the
fly leaves of "Science and Health:"

" I, I, I, I itself, I,
The inside and outside, the what and the why,
The when and the where, the low and the high,
All I, I, I, I itself, I."—*Anonymous.*

I do not wonder that this is *anonymous,* but it is a sample of
much that follows from Mrs. Eddy.

4. The cry for the new. There are many followers of those whom Paul found in Athens, who
" spent their time in nothing else, but either to
tell or to hear some new thing." And while
Christian Science as a philosophy is as old as Bud-
dhism, and as a religion as ancient as Pantheism,
it comes to us to-day clothed in the dress of
modern methods and bedecked with its ribbons
of present-day terminology. Thus it appeals
powerfully to this age, so passionately fond of the
novel and sensational.

5. Predisposition to error. Ever since man
fell from purity into sin his heart has readily
reached out to clasp error and furnished a fruit-
ful soil for its growth. Men love darkness rather
than light, because darkness is in them. They
love error rather than truth, because they contain error. They love wrong, because they are
wrong. The stubborn, rugged truth of God's
word, which tells man that he is a sinner on his
way to hell, is unpalatable to the fallen man.
Therefore he turns from it and embraces the opposite error. " For that they hated knowledge,
and did not choose the fear of the Lord : they
would none of my counsel ; they despised all my
reproof : therefore shall they eat of the fruit of
their own way, and be filled with their own de-
vices " (Prov. i. 29–31). " For the time will come
when they will not endure sound doctrine ; but

after their own lusts shall they heap to themselves teachers, having itching ears; and they
shall turn away their ears from the truth, and
shall be turned unto fables" (2 Tim. iv. 3, 4).
The human mind must have something to rest
on, either facts or fables. I am sure that almost
all infidels have at some time in life willfully
rebelled against the truth, and have therefore
been turned unto the fables of infidelity. And
while I would not bring this sweeping charge
against all who wear the name of Christian
Scientists, yet it is doubtless true of those who
understand its teachings and accept their logical
drift.

May all who have been led into this strangely
fascinating system of error become alarmed and
seek to "recover themselves from the snare of
the devil, who are taken captive by him at his
will."

CHAPTER I.

As a healing art, Christian Science is based on the following syllogism :

> God is all,
> God is spirit ;
> Therefore all is spirit.

Hence there is no matter. What appears to exist outside of mind, is an illusion. This is Idealism pure and simple. But it is easy to make assertions. " To the law and testimony " of the system : " God is all, and God is spirit ; therefore there is nothing but spirit ; and consequently there is no matter " (" Unity of Good," p. 43).

" 1. God is all.

" 2. God is good. Good is mind.

" 3. God, spirit, being all, nothing is matter " (7).

" These verities contradict forever the belief that matter can be actual " (4). " Mind is all, and matter is naught " (3). " Thus matter will be finally proven to be nothing but a mortal illusion, wholly inadequate to affect man through its supposed organic action or existence " (19).

(15)

"Mind in every case is the eternal God, Good" (413).

Even man has no existence except as God or his idea. "Spiritual man is the idea of God, an idea which cannot be lost or separated from its divine Principle" (199). "The Soul, or Mind, of man is God, the divine Principle of his Being" (198). If this is not Idealistic Pantheism, what is it?

The material man has no real existence. "Your mortal body is only a mortal belief of discord. What you call matter was originally primitive error in solution, alias mortal mind" (371). And mortal mind, according to the same authority, is "nothing claiming to be something" (583). All this prepares us for the assertion that God is not the creator of matter: "Hence the Father Mind is not the Father of matter" (153). This is at variance with God's account of creation in Genesis, opening with the sublime sentence, "In the beginning God created the heaven and the earth."

As there is no matter, it reasonably follows there is no disease as a reality, for we have no body to be diseased. A man cannot have liver complaint, for he has no liver. He cannot have a broken arm, for he has no arm. He cannot have headache, for he has no head—and we are tempted to believe this practically true concerning the devotees of Christian Science. Further, there is no disease, because God is all, God is good; therefore all is good, and there can be no disease, for disease is evil. Consequently, even if we had bodies, we could not be sick.

Then, what is disease that has brushed the rosy hue of health from cheeks, bent strong frames and sapped their energy, and made the air in all time past tremulous with wails of pain? Simply an illusion of mortal mind. All sickness and pain are imaginary. In fact, everything is imaginary, except Mind, All, God. Mortal mind itself is an illusion. Therefore disease is an illusion of an illusion. Growing old, weak, weary are illusions. Hunger and thirst are unreal. Death itself is an illusion. Medicine derives its power only from mortal belief and poison works its deadly effect on the same account.

The following quotations from Mrs. Eddy abundantly justify these promiscuous assertions : " Ought we not then to approve any cure affected by making the disease appear to be what it really is—an illusion. Here is the difficulty, that generally it is not understood how one disease is just as much a delusion as another " (294). " Human mind produces what is termed organic disease as certainly as it produces hysteria " (69). "A sick body is evolved from sick thoughts. Evil, disease, and death proceed from false beliefs" (156). " It was scientifically established

2

that leprosy was a creation of mortal mind, and not matter, when Moses first put his hand into his bosom, and drew it forth white as snow with the dread disease, and presently restored his hand to its natural condition, by the same simple process" (217). "Matter cannot be inflamed. Inflammation is an excited stage of mortal mind that is not normal. Immortal mind is the only cause; therefore disease is not a cause or effect. And mind in every sense is the eternal God, Good. Sin, disease, and death have no foundations in Truth" (413). Destruction of the auditory nerve and paralysis of the optic nerve are not needed to insure deafness and blindness; for if mortal mind says, 'I am deaf and blind,' it will be so without any injured nerve" (90). "You say a boil is painful; but that is impossible, for matter without mind is not painful. The boil simply manifests your belief in pain, through inflammation and swelling; and you call this belief a boil" (46, 47). "If a child be exposed to contagion or infection, the mother is frightened, and says, 'My child will be sick.' The law of mortal mind, and her own fears, govern her child, more than her child's mind governs itself, and produce the very results which might have been prevented through the opposite understanding" (48, 49). "The Scientist knows there can be no hereditary disease, since matter can-

not transmit good or evil intelligence to man,
and Mind produces no pain in matter" (411).
"You would not say that a wheel is fatigued;
and yet the body is just as material as the wheel.
If it were not for what the human mind says of
the body, the body would never be weary, any
more than the inanimate wheel" (114). "You
say, or think, because you have partaken of salt
fish, that you must be thirsty, and you are
thirsty accordingly; while the opposite belief
would produce the opposite result" (384).
"This woman learned that food neither strengthens nor weakens the body, though mortal mind
has its material methods of doing this work,
one of which is to declare that proper food sup-
plies nutriment and strength to the human system" (118). Apropos of this, a Christian Scientist told me that he started on a journey by
bicycle early one morning without partaking of
any breakfast. About ten o'clock A.M. he began
to feel hungry; but then he thought, there is
no such thing as hunger, and at once was re-
lieved. About noon he ate dinner and then
pursued his journey, reaching his destination in
the evening, but taking no more food till the
next morning; yet he felt no inconvenience
from hunger. I asked him why he ever ate
again. This stunned him and he had no answer; but the Christian Science teacher, who

was present, was equal to the emergency and said they hoped they would erelong reach the point where they could live without eating, and cited the case of Christ's forty days' fast.

Concerning death Mrs. Eddy says: "The fact that Christ, or Truth, overcame and still overcomes death proves the King of Terrors to be but a mortal belief, or error, which Truth destroys with the spiritual evidences of Life; and this shows that what appears to the senses to be death is but a mortal illusion; for to men, and the spiritual universe, there is no death process" (185). "Jesus said of Lazarus: 'He is not dead, but sleepeth.' He restored Lazarus by the understanding that he had never died, not by an admission that his body had died and then lived again" (241). Yet the record says, "Then said Jesus unto them plainly, Lazarus is dead."

Now note Mrs. Eddy's wisdom concerning drugs: "Mortal mind confers the only power a drug can ever have" (51). "Belief is all that ever enables a drug to cure mortal ailments" (67). "Opiates do not relieve the pain in any proper sense of the word. They only render mortal mind temporarily less fearful" (413). When told that a drug acts when the patient is unconscious, and even when he has no confidence in it, her answer is ready: "When the sick recover, by the use of drugs, it is the law of a general belief, culminating in individual faith, which heals; and according to the faith will the effect be. Even when you take away the individual confidence in the drug, you have not yet divorced it from the general faith. The chemist, the doctor, and the nurse equip the medicine with their faith, and the majority of beliefs rule " (48). " If a dose of poison is swallowed through mistake, and the patient dies, even though physician and patient are expecting favorable results, does belief, you ask, cause the death? Even so, and as directly as if the poison had been intentionally taken. In such cases a few persons believe the portion swallowed by the patient to be harmless; but the vast majority of mankind, though they know nothing of this particular case and this special person, believe the arsenic, the strychnine, or whatever the drug used, to be poisonous, for it has been set down as a poison by mortal mind. The consequence is that the result is controlled by the majority of opinions outside, not by the infinitesimal minority of opinions in the sick chamber " (70).

The question comes, How did drugs and poisons first obtain their particular properties? I think I have seen no answer to this question, but doubtless Mrs. Eddy could readily present one after the idiotic (Eddyotic) nature of the above reasoning.

The inquiry is pertinent, What is "moral mind" which is such a factor in Mrs. Eddy's system, and which she claims is responsible for all our illusions? It is not matter, for that has no existence. It is not spirit, for the object of spirit is to eliminate mortal mind; besides, spirit is good and good only, while mortal mind is evil. Then what is mortal mind? Answer: Nothing; and that is really Mrs. Eddy's teaching. "Mortal mind is a solecism in language, and involves an improper use of the word *mind*. As mind is immortal, the phrase *mortal mind* implies something untrue and therefore unreal; and as the phrase is used in teaching Christian Science it is meant to designate something which has no real existence" (8). "Mortal mind. Nothing, claiming to be something, for Mind is immortal," etc. (583).

It certainly requires more than the fertile imagination of a Kipling to endow Nothing with such genii-like power.

CHAPTER II.

Disease being an illusion, it logically follows the proper method of healing it is by denying its existence and eradicating the erroneous idea from the mind. Christian Scientists do not attempt to heal the sick by prayer. Let no one make the mistake of confounding this system with faith-healing. They are as different as light and darkness. The fact is, Christian Scientists do not believe in prayer in any proper sense. How can they, when God is all and man is simply his idea, or a part of him. It would be praying to one's self. It is true Mrs. Eddy speaks of mental prayer in which the desire is brought unexpressed before God, but even in this she is inconsistent with her system. And not even mental prayer is used in healing the sick. To ask God to heal disease would be to admit its existence, and that admission is exactly what they are trying to eradicate from the mind of the patient. Once the belief that he is sick is lifted from the mind of the patient, he is well, for sickness is only a belief. These assertions are borne out by the following quotations: "If sin, sickness, and death were understood as noth-

(23)

ingness, they would disappear " (476). "Only
through radical reliance on Truth can healing
power be realized" (60). "Disease being a belief, a latent illusion of mortal mind, the sensation would not appear if this error was met and
destroyed by Truth " (61). And truth, according to the system, is to believe in the non-
existence of that which exists. This Truth—
which is error—is the Christian Science GOD.
Mrs. Eddy gives in detail the method which
stamps it, at best, as simply mind-healing:
"Always begin your treatment by allaying the
fear of the patients. Silently reassure the patient as to his exemption from disease and
danger. Watch the result of this simple rule of
Christian Science, and you will find that it alle-
viates the symptoms of every disease. If you
succeed in wholly removing the fear, your patient
is healed. . . . To prevent disease, or to cure
it mentally, let Spirit destroy this dream of
sense. If you wish to heal by argument, find
the type of the ailment, get its name, and array
your mental plea against the physical. Argue
with the patient (mentally, not audibly) that he
has no disease, and conform the argument to the
evidence. Mentally insist that health is the everlasting fact, and sickness the temporal falsity.
Then realize the presence of health, and the
corporeal senses will respond, ' So be it.' If the

case be that of a young child or an infant, it needs to be met mainly through the parents' thought, silently or audibly, on the basis of Christian Science " (410, 411). As an example, she says in dealing with a boil : " Now administer mentally to your patient a high attenuation of truth on this subject, and it will soon cure the boil " (47).

The testimony of the senses is not to be taken relative to disease or anything else, for, according to Mrs. Eddy, they are five liars. " What we term the five physical senses are simply beliefs of mortal mind, which affirm that life, substance, and intelligence are material, instead of spiritual.   These beliefs, and their products, constitute error, and this error opposes the Truth of Being" (170).   " This verdict of the so-called five senses victimizes mortals, taught, as they are by physiology and pathology, to revere those five personal falsities, which are destroyed by Truth, through spiritual sense and understanding" (190).   If the patient says, " I feel pain," he must be assured that that is a lie of the liar called Feeling.   If he says, " I see that my arm has swollen," he must be taught that that is a lie of the lying sense, Sight.   If he says, " I hear my heart beating, and it is irregular," he must learn that it is a lie of the liar, Hearing.

Now, will the reader think for a moment where
we would be without the knowledge gained
through these five senses? They are absolutely
the only avenues of approach between us and all
that is material. All science that pertains to the
earth or its contents, the air, or the worlds that
roll in silent grandeur about us, as well as all
hope of progress in such science, is annihilated
if we accept the teaching of Mrs. Eddy.

To us who believe that God endowed us with
five senses, it is amazing to be asked to believe
that he created " five personal falsities."

Although Christian Scientists do not accept
the testimony of the five senses to sickness, they
do accept it as to healing. If not, how do they
know they are healed at all? But even Mrs.
Eddy accepts it, for we have just read that " the
corporeal senses will respond, ' So be it.' " Now,
if their testimony as to disease is that of five
liars, may it not be that their " So be it " as to
healing is worthless?

Of course, this system *discards* all medicine.
The vast portion of truth that is found in *ma-
teria medica*, the result of thousands of years
of research, is worse than useless. It is harm-
ful, an evil illusion. Physiology is a snare.
The practice of medicine is to be depre-
cated, and " Luke, the beloved physician,"
would not, if he were alive to-day, be an accept-

able applicant for membership in Mrs. Eddy's church. Sanitary science has proved a boon to humanity; yet it is set aside as a silly system of error, and hygiene is a hoax. The war against filth, the cleansing of putrescence, guarding against poisonous atmosphere, the purification of water, are useless measures. All the efforts of the Americans to cleanse the streets, stores, and homes of Santiago of the pestilence of filth that "walketh in darkuess" and "wasteth at noonday" were grievous concessions to error and should never have been made. SURELY THIS IS THE GOSPEL OF FILTH. But, according to Christian Science, there is no filth.

Certainly it is a burlesque to call this a science. It is anti-science, non-science, NONSENSE.

That I have not stated the case too strongly, I make the following quotations: "Medicine is not a science, but a bundle of speculative human theories" (42). "The profession of medicine originated in idolatry, with pagan priests, who besought the gods to heal the sick, and designated Apollo as the God of Medicine. He was supposed to dictate the first prescription, according to the history of Four Thousand Years of Medicine. It is here noticeable that Apollo was also regarded as the sender of disease Hippocrates turned from image-gods to vegetable and mineral drugs for healing. This was

deemed progress, but really it only produced
another form of mythology and pagan worship.
The future fate and history of material medicine
will correspond with that of its material god,
Apollo, who was banished from heaven, and en-
dured great sufferings on earth " (51). "According to my understanding, the sick are never
healed by drugs, hygiene, or any material method.
These merely evade the question. They are
soothing syrups to put children to sleep, satisfy
mortal belief, and lull its fears " (126). " If half
the attention given to hygiene were given to the
study of Christian Science, and its elevation of
thought, this alone would usher in the millen-
nium. Bathing and rubbing, to alter the secre-
tions, or remove unhealthy exhalations from the
cuticle, receive a useful rebuke from Christian
healing. We must beware of making clean
merely the outside of the platter. He who is
ignorant of what is termed hygienic law is more
receptive of spiritual power, and faith in one
God, than the devotee of this supposed law, who
comes to teach him. Must we not then call the
so-called law of matter a canon 'more honored
in the breach than the observance?' . . . .
We need a clean body and a clean mind, a body
rendered pure by mind, not matter. One says,
'I take good care of my body.' No doubt he
attends to it with as much care as he would to

the grooming of his horse; and possibly the
animal sensation of scrubbing has more meaning, to such a man, than the pure and exalting
influence of the divine Mind; but the Christian
Scientist takes the best care of his body when
he leaves it most out of his thought, and, like
the apostle Paul, is ' willing rather to be absent
from the body and present with the Lord ' "
(381, 382). " If exposure to a draught of air,
while in a state of perspiration, is followed by
chills, dry cough, influenza, inflammatory rheumatism, your Mind-remedy is safe and sure. If
you are a Christian Scientist, such symptoms
will not follow from the exposure; but if you
believe in laws of matter, and their fatal effects
when transgressed, you are not fit to conduct
your own case or to destroy the bad effects of
belief. When the fear subsides, and the convic-
tion abides that you have broken no law, neither
rheumatism, nor consumption, nor any other disease will ever result from exposure to the
weather " (383). " We must abandon pharma-
ceutics, and take up ontology, ' the science of
abstract being.' "   " Because the muscles of the
blacksmith's arm are strongly developed, it does
not follow that exercise has produced this result,
or that a less used arm must be weak. If matter were the cause of action, and muscles, without the co-operation of mortal mind, could lift

the hammer and strike the nail, it might be thought true that hammering would enlarge the muscles. The trip hammer is not increased in size by exercise. Why not, since muscles are as material as wood? Because mortal mind is not willing that result on the hammer. Muscles are not self-acting. If mortal mind moves them not, they are motionless. Hence the fact that mortal mind enlarges and strengthens them through its mandate, through its own demand for and supply of power. Not because of muscular exercise, but by reason of the blacksmith's faith in muscle, his arm becomes stronger " (94, 95).*

How unlike the Christian Science mind-cures were those of Christ and his apostles! They recognized disease as a fearful reality and healed it by the power of God. And in some intances, at least, the Bible encourages the use of means, and always the compliance with the laws of health.

---

* What about the infant, the idiot, the brute ?

CHAPTER III.

TENDENCIES.

The attitude of Christian Science towards matter and disease has the following injurious effects in morals:

1. It cultivates inhumaneness. It stifles sympathy for and refuses it to the physically afflicted. How can it be otherwise when the most agonizing protestations of pain are to be met with a complacent denial? The child, whose nerves are all aquiver with suffering, looks up into the eyes of his mother pleading for sympathy, and is smilingly assured by her that he is not suffering. It is all a mistake.

That I do not exaggerate the case will be seen by reading Mrs. Eddy's words: "That mother is not a Christian Scientist, and her affections need better guidance, who says to her child: 'You look sick,' 'You look tired,' 'You need rest,' or 'You need medicine.' Such a mother runs to her little one, who has hurt her face by falling on the carpet, and says, moaning more childishly than her child, 'Mamma knows you are hurt.' The more successful way of treatment is to say: 'Oh, nonsense! You 're not hurt; so do n't think you are.' Presently the child forgets all about the accident and is at play again " (48). Of course, in this supposed hurtless episode there is little harm in this treatment, but it would have been the same, according to the teaching of the whole system, if the child had broken its nose, torn out an eye, or ripped off an ear. How unlike the teachings of Christ, who "took our infirmities and bare our sicknesses," who is "touched with the feeling of our infirmities," and who wept at the grave of Lazarus!

2. It encourages deception. To say you are not sick when you know you are is to lie; yet this is just what Christian Science demands. Many are the subterfuges resorted to by the members of this school to deceive the skeptical. A consumptive Christian Scientist, with whom I was acquainted, was visiting a friend. After she had retired to her room for the night her friend heard her making a strange noise and went in and found her almost suffocated in attempting to smother her coughing. I visited a friend who had been in ill health for years. The disease was consumption. A relative answered my knock. I told her I wished to see Mrs. Blank. I noticed she hesitated, and remarked : " If it is not convenient, I can call again. Is she sick?" "Not to say sick," she whined. Following my request she stepped into another

room to ask the lady if I could see her. On her return her message was, "Not convenient to-day." I seriously suspected that "not to say sick" was a Christian Science misrepresentation. I went to a mutual acquaintance who lived a short distance away and requested her to go and find out the truth. She did so and found the poor woman very sick. She died not long after this. Yet she was "not to say sick."

3. It ignores much of the Bible, and misinterprets much more, and in many instances to such an extent as to virtually dispute its plain teaching. This has been already shown and will be developed more and more in the further treatment of the subject.

3

CHAPTER IV.

Before leaving this department of the treatise it is but due to truth to make the concession that Christian Science does in many instances heal disease. This may be accounted for in the following natural ways:

1. The ills of many people are only imaginary, as Christian Science claims. Their sickness is "all in the mind." Now whatever or whoever eradicates this idea performs a cure.

2. This naturally leads to the further assertion that bodily ailments may be produced by mind and healed through the same instrumentality. A person may imagine himself sick until he *imagines himself sick*, the body sympathizing with the mental state until it really becomes diseased. The preacher may fix his attention on his throat and dwell in such fear of "throat trouble" that irritation will be set up, a cough ensues, and the vocal organs become affected. *Dyspepsia* may be produced by instituting a stomachical inquisition after each meal. It is no surprise then that taking the mind off of these organs and occupying it with something outside the body, leaving them free to perform unmolested their ap-

(34)

pointed functions, results in relief. The effect is all the more potent if the mind firmly grasps the idea that the disease has vanished, for the buoyancy of joy and hope helps the circulation and the action of the nervous system. Every physician recognizes this, and it is a part of his practice.

3. Hypnotism. I am sure that much of the effect of Christian Science practice is due to this agency. I was told by an honored minister of the gospel who graduated from Mrs. Eddy's school, receiving her personal instruction, that this is true. Its power may be seen in the fact that it has been repeatedly employed instead of ether in surgical operations. There are some diseases that will yield to it. I am aware that Christian Scientists deny the practice of it. Some of them doubtless are sincere in such denial, but the influence ofttimes exists when the operator is ignorant of its employment.

But there are cases which are beyond the limit of mind-cure, either as displayed ordinarily or in hypnotism. There are diseases, which not only are not produced by mental action, but exist in spite of belief to the contrary. A tumor may exist for years when the subject is ignorant of it. A baby without belief may be sick. Christian Scientists say that it is the effect of the false belief of the parents; but this is simple idiocy.

Besides, Christian Scientists' babies get sick, and suffer, and die in spite of their parents' belief. The consumptive is characteristically hopeful, and dies disbelieving in his malady, or that he is dangerously ill. A man may be resuscitated from the effects of drowning by immediate and vigorous action, but mind cannot do it. And there are cases in surgery which the mind cannot touch.

A book might be written on the power of mind over matter; its healing efficiency in many instances and its utter futility in others. But I desist and leave this phase of the subject to the physician, for this is his favorite field.

CHAPTER V.

The most injurious effect of Christian Science is in the religious realm. The exposure of the body and refusal of proper treatment and medicine to the sick ofttimes results in physical death, but malpractice with the soul effects its eternal loss. He who deals with souls should walk humbly before God and get wisdom from him who was the model soul-winner. But Mrs. Eddy presumptuously walks in "where angels fear to tread" and dismisses the profoundest question with an oily phrase.

As sin is the tremendous issue with fallen mortals, I will first give the teaching of Christian Science on it. This teaching is based on the following syllogism :

> God is all,
> God is good ;
> Therefore all is good.

Hence there is no sin, or evil effect, or punishment. This is an astounding conclusion. I would not make the assertion without abundant quotations, which I now proceed to give :

(37)

" 1. God is All.

" 2. God is Good.   Good is Mind.

" 3. God, Spirit, being all, nothing is matter.

" 4. Life, God, omnipotent Good, deny death, evil, sin, disease.   Disease, sin, evil, death, deny Good, omnipotent God, Life " (7).

"All that Mind is or hath made is good, and He made all; hence there is no evil " (206).   " Since God is All, there is no room for his opposite. He alone created the real, and it is good; therefore evil, being the opposite of goodness, is unreal, and cannot be the product of God " (234).   " Man is incapable of sin, sickness, and death, inasmuch as he derives his essence from God, and possesses not a single original, or underived, power. Hence the real man cannot depart from holiness " (471). " We shall all learn that sin and mortality are without any actual origin or rightful existence, when we put off the false sense for the true, and see that they have neither principle nor permanency " (177).   " Sin, sickness, and death are comprised in human material belief, and belong not to a divine Mind.   They are without a real origin or existence " (182).   " If Soul could sin,— or be lost, then Being and Immortality would be lost, with all the faculties of Mind; but Being cannot be lost while God exists " (111).   "As for spiritual error, there is none " (187).   Yet Paul speaks of "spiritual wickedness in high

places" (Eph. 6: 12) and "filthiness" of the
spirit as well as of the flesh (2 Cor. 7: 1). Man
is represented as perfect and unfallen: "The
great truth that man was, is, and ever shall be
perfect is incontrovertible" (96). "The Science
of Being reveals man as perfect, even as the
Father is perfect" (198). "The more I understand true humanhood, the more I see it to be
sinless, as ignorant of sin as is the perfect Mak-
er" ("Unity of Good," p. 61). "If man was
once perfect, but has now lost his perfection,
then mortals have never beheld in man the
outlines or realities of divine Mind" (155).
"Through discernment of the spiritual opposite of materiality, even the way through Christ,
Truth, man will reopen, with the key of Science,
the gates of Paradise which human beliefs have
closed, and will find himself unfallen, pure, and
free" (63, 64). The fall is denominated an allegory
(176). The definition of man is, "God's universal idea, individual, perfect, eternal." And
while Mrs. Eddy says, "Man is not God, and
God is not man" (476), yet she also says, "The
Soul, or Mind, of man is God" (198), and as-
sumes his sinlessness therefrom.

As to punishment, she says, "In common jus-
tice, we must admit that God will not punish
man for what he created him capable of doing,

and knew from the outset that he would do"
(302).*

The question arises, What is sin? Mrs. Eddy is ready with an answer. "Nothing is Spirit,
nothing is real and eternal, but God and his idea.
Evil has no reality. It is neither person, place,
nor thing, but is simply a belief, an illusion of
material sense" (237). "They [sin and mortal-
ity] are native nothingness, out of which error
would simulate creation, through a man formed
from dust instead of Deity" (177).

So the world has been laboring under a delusion in considering that sin is a reality, and Mrs.
Eddy's mission is to deliver us from the fright-
ful embrace of this horrible nightmare. Is it
any wonder, then, that Christian Science, by its
devotees, is given a place in advance of the
Church, and Mrs. Eddy more honored than the
apostles or Christ? The following passage from
the leading essay in the June, 1888, number of
the *Christian Science Journal*, illustrates this dis-
position : "That Christian Science is in advance
of the popular churches, no one who has read
without prejudice the wonderful revelations and
indisputable truths of 'Science and Health' can
fail to admit. . . . Creeds and ritualistic modes
of worship retard spiritual advance. The masses

---

* Mrs. Eddy speaks of the suffering incident to sin, but in this
she is inconsistent with her theory.

of church-goers acquiesce in these man-made forms and ceremonies, and lean upon them for support. Creeds are to churches what crutches are to lame men. A lame man can never walk without his crutch until able to abandon it. This is equally true of church creeds and dogmatic assumptions. . . . Our beloved teacher and pastor followed faithfully and devoutly the requirements of the orthodox belief up to the very portal of heaven. Then Christ, hearing her knock for admittance, opened for her a vision of spiritual realities of which mortals had heretofore been ignorant. That spiritual vision is depicted in celestial pictures in ' Science and Health,' whose ' leaves are for the healing of the nations.' John, the revelator, saw this hour. He saw the great wonder which appeared in heaven—a woman clothed with the sun, and the moon under her feet; and upon her head a crown of twelve stars. Who can doubt John's revelation is fulfilled to-day? Surely our beloved pastor is clothed with the sunlight of divine light and love. Moreover, the twelve stars or lights correspond to the twelve pearly gates of the New Jerusalem—gates which open to the twelve tribes of Israel; not the Israel of the flesh, but Israel after the Spirit. The churches of to day hold the same relation to Christian Science that

the law of Moses held to Jesus." This is little
short of blasphemy.

Mrs. Eddy can sit on the hilltop of observation, surrounded by the "illusive" gold which
her fantasies have won her, and look upon the
great river of crime formed by the conjunction
of streams flowing from thousands of wicked
hearts as described in Mark 7: 21, 22, and re-
mark, "All is good; there is no evil. Fornica-
tion, murder, theft, lying, blasphemy, and vile
thoughts are only illusions of mortal mind. Ver-
ily, all is good."

The merest tyro in biblical knowledge knows
that all this contravenes the plain teachings of
the Scriptures on this subject of awful moment
to men. "Lo, this only have I found, that God
hath made man upright; but they have sought
out many inventions" (Eccl. 7: 29). "Where-
fore, as by one man sin entered into the world,
and death by sin, and so death passed upon all
men, for that all have sinned" (Rom. 5: 12).
"Behold, I was shapen in iniquity, and in sin
did my mother conceive me" (Ps. 51: 5). "For
there is no man that sinneth not" (1 Kings 8:
46). "God looked down from heaven upon the
children of men, to see if there were any that
did understand, that did seek God. Every one
of them is gone back; they are altogether become filthy; there is none that doeth good, no,

not one " (Ps. 53 : 2, 3). " But the scripture hath concluded all under sin " (Gal. 3 : 22). " If we say that we have no sin, we deceive ourselves, and the truth is not in us " (1 John 1 : 8). (This marks the Christian Scientist as the deluded one.)

" If we say that we have not sinned, we make him a liar, and his word is not in us " (1 John 1 : 10). " For the wages of sin is death " (Rom. 6 : 23).

CHAPTER VI.

The tremendous question of the ages has ever been, "How shall we get rid of sin?" It has engrossed the concentrated energy of earth's greatest minds. Hundreds of books have been written on it, and many answers have been given. These great minds, pagan and Christian, have discussed it with that deferential carefulness which should characterize all in dealing with that which touches human destiny. It was left for this "modern pope in petticoats," Mrs. Eddy, to suavely tell us that sin is to be got rid of by denying its existence. "To get rid of sin, through Science, is to divest sin of any supposed Mind or reality, and never to admit that sin can have intelligence or power, pain or pleasure. You conquer error by denying its verity. Our various theories will never lose their imaginary power for good or evil until we lose our belief in them, and make Life its own proof of harmony and God" (234, 235). "If sin, sickness, and death were understood as nothingness, they would disappear" (476).

The idea of pardon and cleansing in answer to prayer, as recognized by the Bible, is unknown to Christian Science. "By interpreting God as a corporeal Savior, but not as the saving Prin-

(44)

ciple, we shall continue to seek salvation through pardon, and not through reform, and resort to matter, instead of Spirit, for the cure of the sick" (181). "Prayer cannot change the Science of Being. . . . The habit of pleading with the divine Mind, as one pleads with a human being, perpetuates the belief in God as humanly circumscribed" (308). "The destruction of sin is the divine method of pardon. . . . Being destroyed, sin needs no other form of forgiveness" (234). And, as we have already seen, the way to destroy sin is to deny its existence.

This idea of sin and salvation from it logically leaves no place for Christ's atonement in Mrs. Eddy's system. It is true she says much about it, but only recognizes its effect on the human mind, and even in this she is inconsistent with her theory. She states Christ's mission as follows: "He came to rescue men from these very illusions to which he seemed to conform : from the illusion which calls sin real, and man a sinner, needing a Savior; the illusion which calls sickness real, and man an invalid, needing a physician; the illusion that death is as real as Life. From such thoughts — mortal inventions, one and all—Jesus came to save men, through ever-present and eternal Good" ("Unity of Good," pp. 74, 75). A close inspection of the foregoing language will reveal a great many "illusions."

Stated boldly, the part relative to sin would
read: He came to save men from the illusion
that they need him.   Therefore, instead of coming with the announcement, "God so loved the
world, that he gave his only begotten Son, that
whosoever believeth in him should not perish,
but have everlasting life. . . . He that believeth
on the Son hath everlasting life: and he that
believeth not the Son shall not see life; but the
wrath of God abideth on him" (John 3: 16, 36)
—Mrs. Eddy would have him say, "I come, as
your Savior, to tell you that you do not need
a Savior.   That is an illusion."

In fact, Christian Science teaches that Christ's
death was only seeming.   This must be so to
harmonize with the oft-repeated assertion that
death is an illusion.   "In Science, Christ never
died.   In Sense, Jesus died, and lives again.
The fleshly Jesus seemed to die, though he did
not" ("Unity of Good," p. 78).   Mrs. Eddy
quotes Paul as follows: "For if, when we were
enemies, we were reconciled to God by the [seem-
ing] death of his Son," etc. (351).   It *seems* that
would be a rather *seeming* reconciliation.   How
can anyone read the fifty-third chapter of Isaiah,
and the accounts of Christ's death given by the
evangelists, and say there was anything illusory
about it?

Does not the following convict Mrs. Eddy as
a false prophet?   "Beloved, believe not every

spirit, but try the spirits whether they are of God: because many false prophets are gone out into the world. Hereby know ye the Spirit of God: Every spirit that confesseth that Jesus Christ is come in the flesh is of God: and every spirit that confesseth not that Jesus Christ is come in the flesh is not of God: and this is that spirit of Antichrist, whereof ye have heard that it should come; and even now already is in the world" (1 John 4: 1-3).

The Bible method of getting rid of sin, in opposition to that of Christian Science, is by forgiveness, embracing cleansing by the blood of Jesus. "Forgive us our sins" (Luke 11: 4). "Repent therefore of this thy wickedness; and pray God, if perhaps the thought of thine heart may be forgiven thee" (Acts 8: 22). "That they may receive forgiveness of sin" (Acts 26: 18). "If we confess our sins, he is faithful and just to forgive us our sins, and to cleanse us from all unrighteousness" (1 John 1: 9). "That he by the grace of God should taste death for every man" (Heb. 2: 9). "Much more then, being now justified by his blood, we shall be saved from wrath through him" (Rom. 5: 9). "The blood of Jesus Christ his Son cleanseth us from all sin" (1 John 1: 7). "Unto him that loved us, and washed us from our sins in his own blood" (Rev. 1: 5).

CHAPTER VII.

THE TEACHINGS OF CHRISTIAN SCIENCE ON OTHER SUBJECTS.

Not only is Christian Science astray on sin and salvation, but many other fundamental doctrines.

The Trinity.—The Trinity is denied. "The theory of three persons in one God (that is, a personal Trinity, or Tri-unity) suggests heathen gods, rather than the one ever-present I Am, 'Hear, O Israel, the Lord our God is one Lord'" (152). "Life, Truth, and Love constitute the triune God, or triply divine Principle" (227). Mrs. Eddy denies the Trinity, not as a Unitarian, but as a Pantheist; for we have already seen that she teaches that God is all, and there is nothing that is not God.

By referring to the Bible we find the doctrine of the Trinity clearly revealed. The attributes of personality are ascribed to each, Father, Son, and Holy Spirit; and every convert is to be baptized "in the name of the Father, and of the Son, and of the Holy Ghost."

The Holy Spirit.—The Holy Spirit is defined as "Divine Science; the developments of eternal Life, Truth, and Love" (579). His baptism is made to represent the incoming of a clearer un derstanding. "The magnitude of Jesus' work, his material disappearance before their eyes, his reappearance in idea, all enabled the disciples to understand what Jesus had said. Heretofore they had only believed; now they understood. This understanding is what is meant by the descent of the Holy Ghost—that influx of Divine Science which so illuminated the Pentecostal Day, and is now repeating its ancient history" (348).

Insert Mrs. Eddy's definition of the Holy Spirit in the tender, consoling words of Jesus to his sad apostles, also adapting the pronoun, and note the hollow palaver: "Nevertheless I tell you the truth; it is expedient for you that I go away: for if I go not away, Divine Science will not come unto you; but if I depart, I will send it unto you. . . . Howbeit when it, the Divine Science of truth, is come, it will guide you into all truth: for it shall not speak of itself; but whatsoever it shall hear, that shall it speak: and it will show you things to come" (John 16 : 7, 13).

As to Christ.—Christ is spoken of as an idea, and in harmony with this is referred to as Truth, and stripped of his personality. "As a theoretical life-basis is found to be a misapprehension of existence, the spiritual and divine Principle of man dawns upon human thought, and leads

4

it to 'where the young child lies'—even to the spiritual idea of Life, and what Life includes" (84). "Paul writes, 'If Christ [Truth] be not risen, then is my preaching vain;' that is, If this idea of the supremacy of Spirit, which is the true conception of Being, come not to your thought, you cannot be benefited by what I say" (220). (Can anyone really believe that Paul meant such hollow nonsense?) "If we wish to follow Christ, Truth, it must be in the way of his appointing" (221). "Led by a solitary star amid the darkness, the Magi of old foretold the Messiahship of Truth" (261). It is true she speaks of Christ as a person, and her definition of Christ is, "The divine manifestation of God, which comes to the flesh, to destroy incarnate error" (574). Yet she says almost as much of man.

Origin of Man.—The Bible says, "The Lord formed man of the dust of the ground, and breathed into his nostrils the breath of life; and man became a living soul" (Gen. 2: 7). But Mrs. Eddy calls "the belief that the human race originated materially instead of spiritually —that man started first from the dust, secondly from a rib, and thirdly from an egg," an error. Part of this is doubtless true, but there is enough left of error to contradict the Genesis account. The fact is, Mrs. Eddy teaches the eternity of

man, and therefore that he is without origin.
" Let us remember that the harmonious and immortal man has existed forever " (198). " Both
man and woman proceed from God and are his
eternal children " (521).

Angels.—The Christian Science definition of
angels is, " God's thoughts passing to man, spiritual intuitions, pure and perfect; the inspira-
tion of goodness, purity, and immortality, giv-
ing the lie to evil, sensuality, and mortality "
(572). " They are pure thoughts from God "
(194). " My angels are exalted thoughts. . . .
Angels are God's impartations to man—not *mes-
sengers*, or persons, but *messages* of the true idea
of divinity, flowing into humanity " (195). Now
let us turn to the Bible and *Eddyize* a little. 2
Kings 19: 35—"And it came to pass that night,
that the *pure thought* of the Lord went out and
smote in the camp of the Assyrians an hundred
four score and five thousand." Dan. 6: 21, 22—
" Then said Daniel unto the king, O king, live
forever. My God hath sent his *pure thought*,
and hath shut the lions' mouths, that they have
not hurt me." Rev. 20: 1–3—"And I saw *a pure
thought* come down from heaven, having the
key of the bottomless pit and a great chain in *its*
hand. And *it* laid hold on the dragon," etc.

This is sufficient to render the Christian Science idea of angels ridiculous.

Resurrection.—Christian Science teaches that there is no resurrection of the body, and does away with all resurrection in any Bible sense. "The belief that material bodies return to dust, hereafter to rise up as spiritual bodies, with material sensations and desires, is incorrect" (239). No Bible student would contend for the latter part of this, but Mrs. Eddy's whole theory disputes the blessed fact stated in the first part.

She pumps the obvious meaning out of the Bible texts relative to this doctrine, and then pumps her own hazy idiocy in, that she may pump it out again to harmonize with her general system. The example already given of her emasculation of Paul's noble words, "If Christ be not risen," etc., is illustrative. In harmony with this mental etherialization is her definition of the resurrection: "Spiritualization of thought, a new and higher idea of Immortality, or spiritual existence; material belief yielding to spiritual understanding" (584). All this in the face of plain scripture declaring a literal resurrection of the dead as Christ was raised: "Knowing that he which raised up the Lord Jesus shall raise up us also by Jesus, and shall present us with you" (2 Cor. 4: 14). "The dead in Christ shall rise first" (1 Thess. 4: 16). "And I saw the dead, small and great, stand before God. . . . And the sea gave up the dead which were in it; and death and hell delivered up the dead which were in them: and they were judged every man according to their works" (Rev. 20: 12, 13).

Judgment.—Mrs. Eddy says, "No final judgment awaits mortals" (187). The last quotation under the preceding subject disputes this, besides many other texts. "Because he hath appointed a day in the which he will judge the world in righteousness" (Acts 17: 31). "For we must all appear before the judgment seat of Christ" (2 Cor. 5: 10). "After this the judgment" (Heb. 9: 27). Lack of space forbids other quotations, and particularly that sublime description of the final judgment scene in Matt. 25: 31–46.

Hell.—Mrs. Eddy has no place in her invertebrate system for the scripture doctrine of hell. She speaks of it, but only to filch from it its awful meaning. Her definition is as follows: "Mortal belief; error; lust; remorse; hatred; sin; sickness; death; suffering and self-destruction; self-imposed agony; effects of sin; that which maketh and worketh a lie" (579). When we remember that all these are illusions, hell is seen to be a very attenuated doctrine in Christian Science. In fact, she teaches an after-death probation theory which excludes the Bible idea of hell. "As man falleth asleep, so shall he awake. As death findeth mortal man, so shall he be after death, until probation and growth shall effect the needful change " (187). "Those who reach the transition called *death*, without having rightly improved the lessons of this primary school of mortal existence, and still believe in matter's reality, pleasure, and pain, are not ready to understand Immortality. Hence they awake only to another sphere of experience, and must pass through another probationary state before it can be truly said of them, ' Blessed are the dead that die in the Lord ' " ("Unity of Good," p. 3).

In opposition to this, the Bible says : " The wicked shall be turned into hell, and all the nations that forget God " (Ps. 9 : 17). Jesus said : "And if thy hand offend thee, cut it off: it is better for thee to enter into life maimed than having two hands to go into hell, into the fire that shall never be quenched : where their worm dieth not, and their fire is not quenched " (Mark 9 : 43, 44). "And these shall go away into everlasting punishment" (Matt. 25 : 46).

Heaven.—Christian Science teaches erroneously about heaven, viz.: That it is not a place, but simply a harmonious state of mind. "Heaven is not a locality, but a state in which Mind, and all the manifestations of Mind, are harmonious and immortal " (187). The definition given of heaven is, "Harmony ; the reign of Spirit ;

government by Principle; spirituality; bliss; the atmosphere of Soul" (578).

Jesus says: "In my Father's house are many mansions: if it were not so, I would have told you. I go to prepare a place for you. And if I go and prepare a place for you, I will come again, and receive you unto myself, that where I am, there ye may be also" (John 14: 2, 3).

Devil.—Christian Science teaches the most erroneous v i e w s concerning the devil and demons. The devil is error and demons are evil beliefs. The definition of devil is, "Evil; a lie; error; neither corporeality nor mind; the opposite of truth; a belief in sin, sickness, and death; animal magnetism," etc. (575).* "This pantheistic error, first called the *serpent*, insists still on the opposite of Truth" (202, 203). "There are evil beliefs, often called evil Spirits; but these evils are not Spirit, or they could not be evil. There is no evil in Spirit" (102). Hence wherever the Bible speaks of Christ's casting out devils, Mrs. Eddy reads it "evils," or "error." Example: "Christ healed the sick and cast out error" (63). "Healing the sick, casting out error" (106). "Jesus cast out evil and healed the sick" (79).

---

*It is remarkable that the definition of Adam, made in the likeness of God, is substantially the same: "Error; a falsity; the belief in 'original sin,' sickness, and death; evil," etc. (570).

As evil, according to Christian Science, is an illusion, Mrs. Eddy is consistent with herself when she concludes that Satan is an illusion: " The beliefs of the human mind rob and enslave it, and then impute this result to another illusive personification, named Satan " (81).

It is almost superfluous to say that the Bible teaches that Satan and demons are spiritual intelligences, clothing them with the attributes of personality. See Job 1 : 6-12; Matt. 4: 1-11; 1 Pet. 5: 8, 9. Relative to demons the following references are pertinent: Mark 5: 1-13; Matt. 15: 22-28; Luke 11: 14-20.

Death in the Next World.—Notwithstanding Christian Science teaches that death is a delusion, yet, strange to say, it is given a place in the next world: " Death will occur on the next plane of existence as on this, until the understanding of Life is reached " (243).

CHAPTER VIII.

FALSE HERMENEUTICS.

I think enough has been said to prove that Christian Science would undermine the foundations of Christian faith, and emasculate the Bible, and make it appear a series of thinly connected vagaries. But, to render this assertion still more apparent and impressive, I append the following examples of f a l s e hermeneutics : " Jacob was *alone*, wrestling with error—struggling with a mortal sense of life, substance, and intelligence as existent in matter, with its false pleasures and pains—when an angel, a message from Truth and Love, appeared to him, and smote the sinew, or strength, of his error, till he became powerless; and God, being thus understood, gave him spiritual strength in this Peniel of Divine Science. Then said the spiritual evangel : ' Let me go, for the day breaketh ; ' that is, The light of Truth and Love dawns upon thee ; but the Patriarch, perceiving his own error and need of help, did not loose his hold upon this glorious light until his nature was transformed. When Jacob was asked, ' What is thy name?' he straightway answered ; and then his name was changed to Israel, for ' as a prince '

(57)

had he prevailed, and had 'power with God and with men.' Then Jacob questioned his deliverer, 'What is *thy* name?' but this appellation was nameless and withheld, for the messenger was not a corporeal being, but an incorporeal impartation of God to man, which, to use the word of the Psalmist, *restored* his soul—gave him the true Sense of Being and rebuked his material sense" (204, 205).

Here are some expositions of passages in Genesis:

1: 6. "Let there be a firmament in the midst of the waters, and let it divide the waters from the waters."

"Understanding is the spiritual firmament, whereby human conception distinguishes between Truth and error" (499).

1: 8. "And God called the firmament heaven. And the evening and the morning were the second day."

"Spirit unites understanding to eternal harmony through Divine Science. The calm and exalted thought takes upon itself understanding, and is at peace; while the dawn of ideas goes on, forming the second stage of progress" (500).

1: 9. "And God said, Let the waters under the heaven be gathered together unto one place, and let the dry land appear."

"Spirit gathers unformed thoughts into their

proper channels. God unfolds these thoughts, even as he opens the petals of a rose, to send their fragrance abroad " (500).

2 : 21, 22. "And the Lord God caused a deep sleep to fall upon Adam, and he slept: and he took one of his ribs, and closed up the flesh instead thereof. And the rib, which the Lord God had taken from man, made he a woman, and brought her unto the man."

" Here falsity, error, charges Truth, God, with inducing a hypnotic state in Adam, in order to perform a surgical operation on him, and thereby to create woman. Beginning creation with darkness instead of light—materially rather than spiritually. Error now simulates the work of Truth, mocking Love and declaring what great things error hath done. Beholding the creations of his own dream, and calling them real and God-given, Adam, *alias* error, gives them names. Afterwards he becomes the basis of the creation of woman, and of his own kind, calling them *mankind*" (521).

The red dragon (Rev. 12: 3) is defined as " Fear; inflammation; sensuality; subtlety; error; animal magnetism " (584).

" When a new spiritual idea is borne to earth, the prophetic scripture of Isaiah is renewedly fulfilled : ' Unto us a child is born, . . and his name shall be called Wonderful " (3).

" In Egypt it was Mind which saved the Israelites from the belief in plagues " (26).

Therefore we conclude, whatever Christian Science may or may not be, it is not Christian. Let it be honest. Let it no more parade before the world with the Bible in one hand and " Science and Health " in the other, and under the cross the actuality of which it disputes. Let it trample the Bible under foot and tear the sacred name, " Christian," from its banner. Let it call itself Idealistic Pantheism, or Mental Therapeutics, or Occultism, or Eddyism, but let it be honest and drop the name Christian.

CHAPTER IX.

A PERTINENT QUESTION.

What would be the effects of the universal acceptance of the doctrines of " Eddyism," as they relate to matter and spirit? This is a pertinent question. Let us " look before we leap."

First, as to matter. All knowledge concerning it would be accounted obsolete and worthless, and worse still: error. Chemistry, anatomy, geology, astronomy, and kindred sciences would be no more taught in our schools, for they have to do with that which has no existence. Special condemnation would fall on medical colleges, and the vast reservoir of therapeutic and sanitary knowledge, the accumulation of the wisdom of the ages, would be considered the Valley of Hinnom (the type of hell) outside the Jerusalem of *Eddyistic* harmony. In fact, all schools would be turned into *Eddy* churches, where *Eddy* preachers, with vague stare and idiotic complacency, and hollow, oily bombast, would assure their hearers, over and over, *ad infinitum, ad nauseam,* "All are well; there is no disease. All is good; there is no sin."

Mrs. Eddy says, "Knowledge gained from matter, or through the material senses, is only

(61)

an illusion of mortal mind—the offspring of bodily sense, not of Soul, Spirit—and symbolizes all that is evil and perishable. *Natural Science*, as it is commonly called, is not really natural or scientific, because it is deduced from the evidence of the physical senses" (170).

Second, the effect in the spiritual realm would be even worse. Let the world accept the doctrine that there are no sin and sinners, and that mind does not err, and the barriers of morality are gone and the evil of the human heart is given unbridled license. For if there can be no evil there is no moral law, the standard by which to pattern human life. And without moral law ethical distinctions are obliterated and moral chaos is the inevitable doom.

The reader may this moment be thinking of some devout *Eddyite* and placing him as a refutation of the foregoing. I grant readily there are such. But they may be accounted for as follows:

1. They may not accept understandingly the whole of Mrs. Eddy's system.

2. The effect of Christian training still holds sway.

3. The false doctrines have not yet wrought out their logical tendency. On account of former religious teaching they may never do so in these particular persons. But wait a generation

or two, until the old landmarks are wiped out, and the influence of our fathers' faith is dead, and see the logic of the case consummated in their descendants. There can be but one final result of the universal denial of the existence of sin, and that is its complete sway and the destruction of good. Would it be safe to teach our children that they cannot commit evil? Would it be safe for society? Would it be safe for the state? Would it be safe for the world? Would it be safe for time? Would it be safe for eternity? All human experience, observation, and reason, and the Bible, answer in unison, *No!*

We are forced to the conclusion stated in the title, that Christian Science is *neither Christian nor scientific,* and further, it is anti-Christian and anti-scientific.

My friend, beware of the teaching of Eddyism. Be not deceived by the relation of their wonderful cures, or their assumption of superior knowledge or piety. Wonder working is not the test of divineness. Paul speaks of one "whose coming is after the working of Satan, with all power and signs and lying wonders." Jesus said, "Take heed that no man deceive you. For many shall come in my name, saying, I am Christ; and shall deceive many. . . . And many false prophets shall rise, and shall deceive many. And because iniquity shall abound, the love of many shall wax cold. . . . For there shall arise false Christs, and false prophets, and shall show great signs and wonders; insomuch that, if it were possible, they shall deceive the very elect" (Matt. 24: 4, 5, 11, 12, 24).

Cling to the *Old Book*, " *The impregnable rock of the Holy Scriptures*," with its old meaning infused into it and made plain by the Holy Spirit. Stand by the old doctrines that caused our fathers to flee sin and hell as awful realities and escape them through faith in Christ and cleansing by his blood. And let the old, old story of the cross, the "hope of earth and joy of heaven," be ever fresh upon your lips.

www.ingramcontent.com/pod-product-compliance
Lightning Source LLC
Chambersburg PA
CBHW021522090426
42739CB00007B/741